GW00776750

FIBRES

Contributory Author
Brian Knapp, BSc, PhD
Art Director
Duncan McCrae
Special photography
Graham Servante
Special models
Tim Fulford, Head of CDT, Leighton Park School
Editorial consultants
Anna Grayson, Rita Owen
Science advisor
Jack Brettle, BSc, PhD, Chief Research Scientist, Pilkington plc
Environmental Education Advisor
Colin Harris, County Advisor, Herts. CC
Production controller
Patricia Browning
Print consultants
Landmark Production Consultants Ltd
Printed and bound in Hong Kong

Designed and produced by
EARTHSCAPE EDITIONS

First published in the United Kingdom in 1991
by Atlantic Europe Publishing Company Ltd,
86 Peppard Road, Sonning Common, Reading,
Berkshire, RG4 9RP, UK

Copyright © 1991
Atlantic Europe Publishing Company Ltd

677

British Library Cataloguing in Publication Data

Knapp, Brian
  Fibres
  1. Fibres – For children
  I. Title   II. Series
  677

ISBN 1-869860-20-9

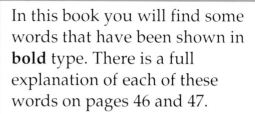

In this book you will find some words that have been shown in **bold** type. There is a full explanation of each of these words on pages 46 and 47.

On many pages you will find experiments that you might like to try for yourself. They have been put in a coloured box like this.

Acknowledgements
The publishers would like to thank the following:
Becky Briscoe, Irene Knapp, Leighton Park
School, Janet McCrae, Martin Morris,
Micklands County Primary School,
Stephen Pitcher, Redlands County
Primary School and Royal Berkshire
Fire and Rescue Service.

Picture credits
t=top b=bottom l=left r=right

All photographs from the Earthscape Editions
photographic library except the following:
Aquila 18t; Bruce Coleman Ltd 8b;
Fire Research Station 37t; Hutchison
Library 22, 29t, 44; NASA 36.

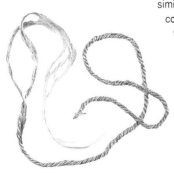

Contents

Introduction

fur
page 8

seed fibres
page 16

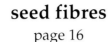

weaving
page 26

clothing
page 44

Put your hand to your head and feel your hair. Put your hand on your clothes and feel their touch. Both hair and clothes are made of long thin strands. We call these strands **fibres**.

There are so many fibres in the world that many of them have special names. The fibres are twisted together to form long strands. These **yarns** can be criss-crossed, or woven, to make **textiles** like cloth or **fabric**. On this page you can see some of the variety of fibres and their uses. You may not even have believed some were fibres at all!

hair
page 6

synthetics
page 18

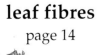

wool uses
page 32

dyes
page 38

leaf fibres
page 14

nets
page 28

Fibres come from many different sources. Many come from plants: the cotton of a shirt, the mat by our front doors, the paper of this book. Some others come from animals: the hair on our heads, the fur of a seal, even the horn of a rhinoceros. Other fibres have been made entirely by people and do not occur in nature. The nylon used for ropes or the fibres used to make many types of clothes are made by people.

In this book you can discover the fascinating variety of fibres in any way you choose. Just turn to a page and begin your discoveries.

What is hair ?

Hair is one of the most common materials found in nature. We have hair all over our bodies, not just on our heads.

We have eyebrows and eye-lashes made of short stiff hairs, but we also have tiny hairs all over our bodies. Each set of hairs is not there by accident; it has a special job to do.

The hair on our heads

The hair on our heads helps to protect us from the scorching heat of a summer sun or the freezing cold of winter.

Hairstyle

By changing your hairstyle you can change the way head hair works for you.

If you have short hair, or keep it tied up over your head, then you can keep cooler in warm weather.

If you have long hair or let it fall round your head, you get better protection in the cold.

Are there other ways you can use your hair?

How hair is made

Hair grows out of tiny **pores** in the surface of our skin. Just below the skin new hair is made from **cells** in our bodies. As it is pushed through the surface, so it is given a special coating that makes it go hard and stiff. The cells in hair are dead. This is the reason it does not hurt if we cut our hair.

Straight or curly?

Some people have straight hair. Others have very curly hair. The type of hair you have depends on its shape.

If you have straight hair then your hairs are round and rod-like. It is hard to curl a rod. But if you have curly hair this means your hairs are flatter, and they can curl up – just like a watch spring.

Look at some strands of hair through a good magnifying glass to see if they are round or flat.

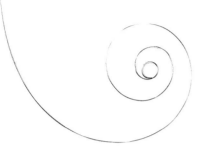

Eyebrows

Eyebrows help to shade our eyes. They are made of medium length hair which is rod-shaped and so tends to stay straight

Hair that stands on end

The hair on your arms normally lies close to your skin. But if you put cold water or an ice cube on your arm the hairs stand on end. This is nature's age-old way of trying to protect us from the cold.

Eyelashes

Eyelashes partly shade our eyes but they also help keep dirt and dust out. They have to stay stiff, so they are quite thick as well as being rod-shaped

Nose hairs

You do not normally notice the hairs in your nose, but they have a very important job to do.

If you look carefully in a mirror you will see there are tiny hairs just inside your nose. They stick out from the inside wall and cross over to make a kind of net.

The job of these hairs is to stop unwelcome things such as dust, soot or flies from being drawn in by your nose as you breathe in

Furry coats

Many animals are covered with thick hair called **fur**. You see a squirrel on a branch with its fine grey fur and bushy tail. You glimpse a fox disappearing into the woods. Each of them has a special type of thick furry coat.

All furry coats help trap air and keep animals warm. But you will soon realise that fur coats may have many uses.

Squirrel tail

This is the tail of a squirrel. Notice that its hairs are long. By bushing out its tail it can trap air and keep warm in cold weather. However, the long hairs have other uses. They also help the squirrel to keep balance as it jumps from branch to branch by making the tail heavier. Notice how this grey squirrel drapes its tail over the branch to help it keep balance while eating.

Fur for the job

Squirrels live in many places. Some, like the red and grey squirrels, live in trees, while others, like the chipmunk and marmot, live in burrows in the ground.

The ground squirrel's fur is fine and lies close to its body. This helps it get in and out of burrows easily. The tree squirrel uses its long bushy fur to keep warm in its exposed tree-hollow nest.

Squirrel

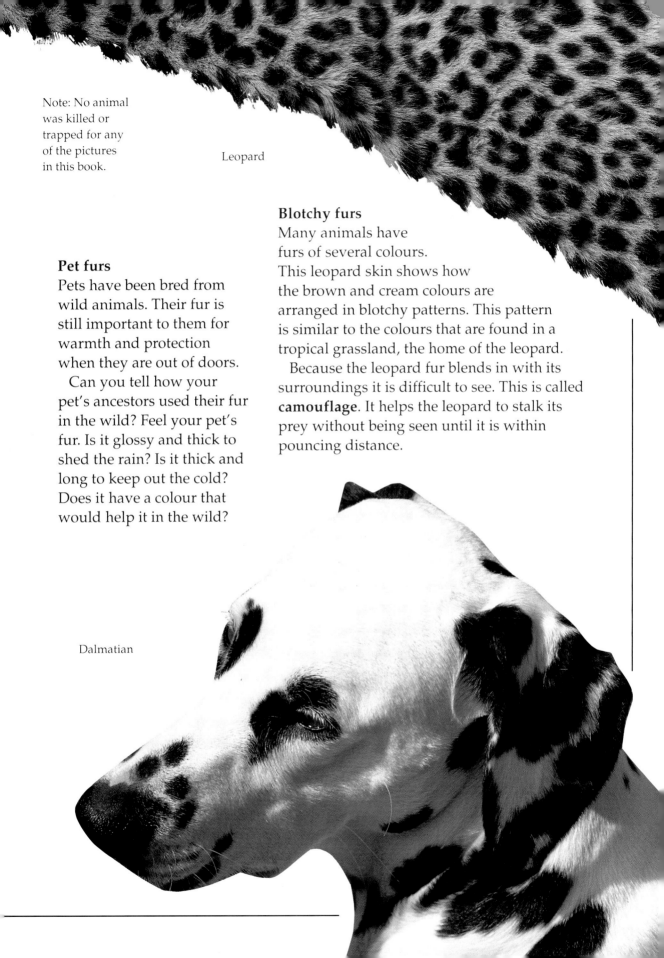

Leopard

Blotchy furs

Many animals have
furs of several colours.
This leopard skin shows how
the brown and cream colours are
arranged in blotchy patterns. This pattern
is similar to the colours that are found in a
tropical grassland, the home of the leopard.

Because the leopard fur blends in with its
surroundings it is difficult to see. This is called
camouflage. It helps the leopard to stalk its
prey without being seen until it is within
pouncing distance.

Pet furs

Pets have been bred from
wild animals. Their fur is
still important to them for
warmth and protection
when they are out of doors.

Can you tell how your
pet's ancestors used their fur
in the wild? Feel your pet's
fur. Is it glossy and thick to
shed the rain? Is it thick and
long to keep out the cold?
Does it have a colour that
would help it in the wild?

Dalmatian

Fibres from hair

The hair, or fur, from many animals can be used to make all manner of materials.

Wool holds a special place. For thousands of years people and sheep have lived side by side; people protecting the sheep from foxes and wolves, the sheep providing people with food and wool.

This **fleece** contains 8000 kilometres of wool fibre.

A fleece has millions of fibres packed side by side as the picture shows.

Wool machine

The wool fibres on a sheep grow at a rate of just two hundredth of a centimetre a day. But each sheep has a hundred million fibres growing on its body.

Add all the tiny growths together and you discover that a sheep is growing wool at a kilometre an hour. That's over 8000 kilometres a year. Australia, the world's largest wool producing country, has over 150 million sheep. Together the sheep produce enough wool fibre to stretch from the Earth to the Sun 8000 times!

Shearing

Sheep have thick coats to keep them warm in the winter. Many breeds lose their coats, or fleeces, each summer; their wool falling away or moults in clumps and tufts.

Picking the tufts of the sheep is time-consuming, although it is still done in many countries. To save time and effort most farmers with large flocks shear sheep. It's just like having your hair cut.

The curly nature of the wool helps to hold the fleece together as it is being cut. A skilled shearer aims to get the whole fleece off in one piece.

Any old wool?

There are over a thousand breeds of sheep in the world, each with its own special type of wool. Some wool, such as that from Scottish mountain sheep, is coarse and grey in colour. Others are incredibly fine.

The most numerous sheep is the merino. This breed supplies over a third of the world's wool. Each strand of wool is five times as fine as a human hair.

Luxurious cashmere and mohair

Cashmere and **mohair** are the finest wools. They are made from the soft undercoat of Himalayan goats.

This fine wool is very fragile and has to be blended with other wool to make a yarn. Some of this wool is so fine that an entire shawl can be pulled through a wedding ring!

Kashmir goats on a mountainside in the Kashmir Himalayas. The Cashmere is the undercoat wool.

Silk: spinning a line

In the world of fabric, a humble caterpillar can do what people cannot. Although there are many man-made fibres in the world, none comes close to the look and feel of silk.

It seems strange that the most expensive fabric in the world should be produced by a small white caterpillar.

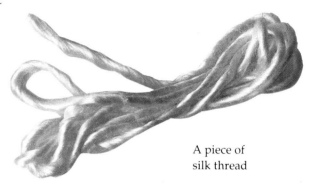

A piece of silk thread

The shape of silk
While nearly all other fibres are round, the silk produced by the caterpillar is triangular in shape. When light shines on any of its three flat surfaces it bounces off, making the silk shine.

A silken cocoon
Silk is made by the silkworm. However it is not a worm at all, but a caterpillar of a moth.

As the caterpillar begins the process of change to a moth it must first build a **cocoon**. It does this by producing silk from a special place in its head.

It begins to build its home as one long thread, rolling itself round and round thousands of times until it is completely wrapped up. The single thread produced may be up to two kilometres long.

Turning a cocoon into a thread

To get the silk from a cocoon people put the cocoons in tubs of hot water. This softens the glue-like substance that covers the silk and allows people to pick up the threads and unwind them in long strands.

Silk finds

You can make a pin cushion like the one shown below by pulling a piece of silk over a ball of cotton wool and then sewing the ends together tightly.

Try pushing some pins into this kind of pin cushion. Can you see how its special shiny fibres are useful for getting pins in and out without damaging the material?

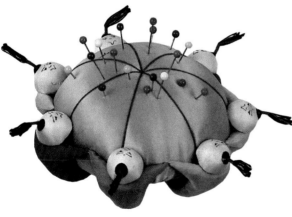

How many cocoons are you wearing?

Although the thread from each cocoon is so long, it takes a large number of cocoons to make even small items of cloth.

A silk tie, such as the one shown here, may need over 100 cocoons and a blouse may use over 600.

The fine cloaks called kimonos that are worn in East Asia, may need over 3000 cocoons.

Fibres from stems and leaves

This traditional Thai hat is made from palm tree fibres

Many of the commonest plants in your garden have stems and leaves that are made from fibres. Some plants have such strong fibres that they are almost impossible to break from the plant.

Plants with tough stems or leaves are made of lots of long fibres, so when you try to break these stems it is almost like trying to break a rope.

Stringy greens

If plant stems are boiled the fibres often come apart. Ask a grown-up to help you to cook some stems of garden weeds like nettles (cut the stinging leaves away first); you will see that the stems go soft. When the cooked stems are cool, try picking the fibres from the stem by hand.

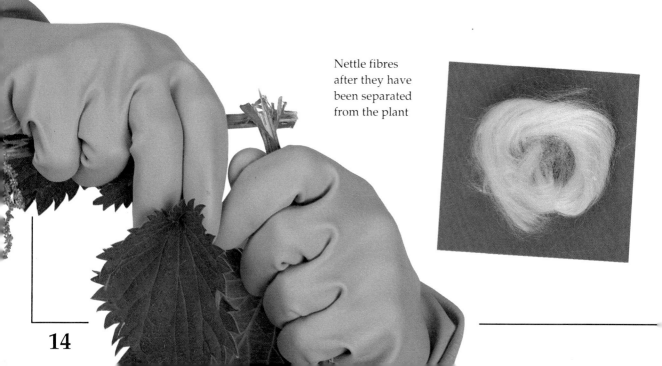

Nettle fibres after they have been separated from the plant

Hemp was used for
waterproofing joints in
pipework as well as for ropes

Jute, hemp and flax

Many plants have long stems made from
strong fibres. Jute, hemp and flax are all
fibres that come from the stalks of plants.

When the stalks are cut they are soaked in
water so that the outer skin can be removed.
Next the inner fibres are separated out by machines.

Flax produces linen, a tough fabric not unlike
cotton. As hemp is slow to rot it is used to make
ropes. Jute is used for making sacks and is very coarse.

Raffia

Raffia is made from the very long broad leaves of
a tropical palm tree. The leaves are up to 20 metres
long and they have to be strengthened with tough
fibres if they are to stand up to the fierce battering
of a tropical storm.

Each main leaf is made from up to 100 narrow
leaflets. The leaflets are torn into long thin shreds
and left to dry in the sun.

Raffia will not shrink and its long fibres are
difficult to break.

Most grasses in your garden also have long thin
leaves, but they are too brittle to use like raffia.
This is because the fibres are shorter and weaker.

Jute sacking

Raffia as
garden twine

Raffia used
in basketry

Fibres from seeds

Some plants have fluffy seeds. The fluffy material is made of fibre.

Many of the plants in your garden have seeds with fibres. Watch the dandelion 'parachutes' as they are blown away from a seed head. Each parachute has many fine downy fibres. However, although there are literally thousands of plants that produce seed fibres, only a few have fibres that are really useful.

Parachutes from a dandelion head

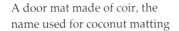

A door mat made of coir, the name used for coconut matting

Coconut

Coconuts hide their fibre inside a green pod. This fibre pod is called a husk and it protects the brown nut. The nut is the coconut (seed) you buy in the shops.

To harvest the fibre the pod has to be split open and the seed taken out. Then the fibre can be stripped from the husk.

The brown coarse fibre is tough and makes good matting.

Picking cotton in the fields of Botswana

Cotton

By far the most useful of all fibre plants is cotton. Raw cotton is picked from the seed pod or cotton boll of the cotton bush.

Cotton plants grow in countries that have hot moist summers. The cotton boll is pure white and it forms after the flowers have faded away.

When the cotton boll is ripe the tufts of fibre burst out and produce a loose ball of white cotton.

Cleaning cotton

Natural cotton fibres are all mixed up, or matted, and attached to the seeds. The seeds have to be pulled from the fibres and the fibres all made to lie the same way.

Separating seeds from cotton fibre (called lint) is done by machines that have long teeth, like combs. As one set of combs put the cotton through narrow slots, the seeds are pulled off. Then the fibres are untangled with a machine that works rather like a hair brush.

After the cotton has been untangled it can be spun into thread like the ones shown below.

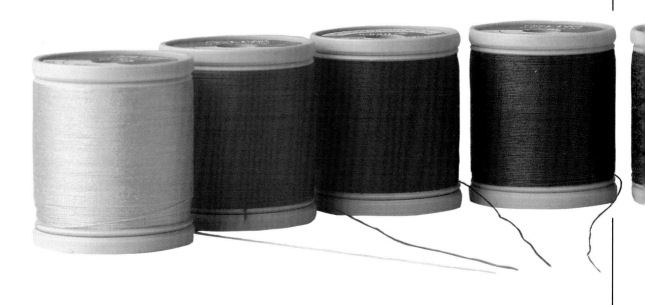

Design a fibre

People have always wanted to copy the effortless way a spider or a silkworm make their threads.

Today scientists can design fibres to meet a range of needs. Each artificial fibre is called a synthetic fibre.

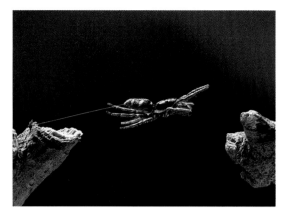

Designed for use
Skiing gloves have to be very warm and waterproof. The surface must be tough to stand up to rubbing by the ski sticks.

Ski gloves are often made from two different types of the same man-made fibre called **polyester**.

The spider's trick
The spider makes its thread as a liquid inside its body. As the thread is forced out (extruded) from a special place on its body, it hardens. The hardened thread is immediately tough and flexible.

Factories all over the world try to copy the spider's trick as they make artificial fibres.

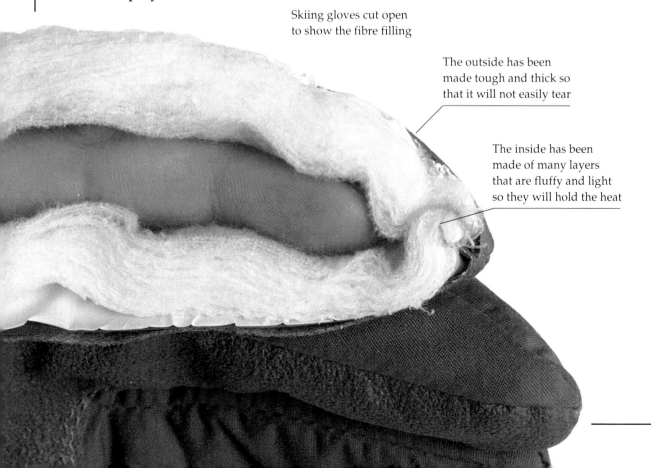

Skiing gloves cut open to show the fibre filling

The outside has been made tough and thick so that it will not easily tear

The inside has been made of many layers that are fluffy and light so they will hold the heat

The ordinary-looking material shown above is Kevlon. It is a special substance that is so tough it cannot be cut with scissors. It is used to make lightweight bullet-proof vests for the police and soldiers in the army.

Rayon
The building blocks of plant fibre are made of a simple substance called cellulose. By special methods the cellulose can be extracted from plants and then made up into a new fibre that does not exist in nature. This fibre is called rayon (or sometimes viscose).

Nature and man-made together
Wool and polyester is a mixture often used for coats, jackets and trousers. Can you think why this might make good sense? Look at the labels on your clothes and other items such as sheets. Can you find other mixtures of materials?

Glass fibre is made by melting glass and then forcing it through small holes so that it makes a long thread. The threads are then often used to make glass-fibre matting. Glass fibres mats are coated with special glues called resins to make strong shapes such as canoes

Rot-proof fibre
Nylon was the first fibre to be made from oil. It is very strong and lightweight. Now there are hundreds of others, each with its own special use.

This is carbon fibre. It is very tough and is used in aeroplanes and racing cars where tough and lightweight materials are needed.
  Carbon is the main substance in coal and oil.

Secrets of paper

Paper has many of the same properties as fabric. Paper can also be made with a fine surface and it can easily be printed to give newspapers and books. It will bend and flex and it is strong. This is because it is made out of fibres.

What is paper made of?
Paper is made of fibre. Just about half of the fibre comes from trees that have been cut down specially for papermaking. But the rest comes from recycling paper, old cartons and packaging; old straw and stalks from farms; and waste cotton from cotton mills. All of these materials will make paper of varying qualities. Some fibre for making paper even comes from old rags. Just think, you may now be reading your old clothes!

Felting
Felting is the process of matting fibres together. If matted fibres are pressed together hard they give a very dense material. One such material is paper.

To get fibres to mat into paper they have to be cooked and stirred in a giant liquidiser for many hours. Then they are bleached to make them white.

Chalk or china clay are added to give a smooth texture. The mixture is turned out onto large flat sieves and the water pressed out to make a sheet of paper.

Straw

Coloured rag

Spruce chippings

Paper takes over

Paper is used in many new ways. For example, the paper fibres can be pulled or **teased** out so they only mat loosely together. When this is done the paper absorbs water easily.

Kitchen spills are often cleared up by absorbent paper towels because they are cheap and they can be hygienically and easily disposed of or recycled.

Paper handkerchiefs

All fibres absorb water, but if they are fluffed up they will absorb much more.

Look at a paper handkerchief and see how it is made of layers.

Try pulling it apart and you will see that each layer has its fibres laid in a different direction. The layers make it strong and they also allow the water to be held – just like a sponge.

(For more information on paper making and recycling fibres including paper see Science in our World, 'Don't throw it away')

Giving fibres a twist

Single fibres are very weak, but when they are twisted together they make much stronger threads. Sometimes different fibres are mixed or blended together to make the thread even more hard wearing. The age-old craft of **spinning** is used to twist fibres to produce very long threads for knitting, sewing or weaving.

String

Whenever you want to tie up a parcel or to hold something together, you use string.

String is often made from jute, although it can be made from nylon and even paper. It is tougher than a thread, and cheaper too. It's also easier to handle because it is thicker.

Spinning

Spinning can be done by hand or machine. Hand spinning is still common in countries like Peru in South America. Spinning is done using a spindle, which is spun like a top to put twist into the fibres to make a thread.

Most factory spinning is done on very fast automatic machines. The 'Spinning Jenny' is the name of one of a spinning machine invented in 1766. It helped to start the factory age.

Hand spinning in Peru

Yarns

Many people think of yarns when they think of kitting. Knitting yarns normally come either in long loose rolls called **skeins**, or more tightly packed into balls. These are convenient for both hand and machine knitting.

Jute string

A wool skein

Ropes

Ropes are the giants among twisted fibres. They are often made of hemp or nylon. Millions of fibres are spun together so that they are strong and will not break.

Rope tricks

Fibres are at their strongest when they are all lying in the same direction. This is the reason people make ropes. But a single bundle of threads is stiff, weak and not at all easy to use. Big ropes are always therefore made of plaited or twisted threads.

Plaiting

Plaiting is a good way to make a rope. Tie three pieces of string together at one end and put this end over a hook such as a coat hook. Now lay one string over another in order as shown. Keep the strings stretched taut.

When you have used up all the string the plait is complete. It is really a rope. Try using it to pull objects or to tie parcels. Work out some differences in properties between string and plaited rope.

Ropes with stretch

Ropes are often used to hold boats against the quayside. These ropes have great strength, but they are also flexible. This lets them hold the boats in place as the tide rises and falls.

How to make a rope or cord

Ropes look simple to make, so why not try it for yourself. This grandfather from India shows how it is done.

First take a number of pieces of coarse string about 30 centimetres long and tie them at one end. Now sit cross legged on the floor and hook the tied end over your big toe!

Take the free ends and put them side by side in the palms of your hands. Then run one palm over the other quickly again and again so that you twist the strings together.

A finished rope is shown in close up. All the threads are just twisted together.

The rope made by the man in the picture. Notice how it is made from many strands.

Loops and lacings

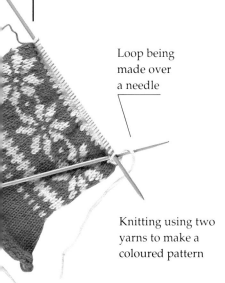

Loop being made over a needle

Knitting using two yarns to make a coloured pattern

Clothes, carpets, sails and tents – in fact all fabrics – are made from threads. There are few knots or joins. The threads do not fall apart because they have been interlaced, or **woven**, into a pattern.

There are other ways to interlace threads, the most common of these is **knitting**, a way of interlocking loops.

Knitting

Knitting uses *one* strand of a yarn and is formed into *loops* that are interlocked with one another using a pair of needles.

Many modern fabrics are knitted. Lots of people knit by hand at home. Different textures of the knitting are made by changing the thickness of the yarn and by changing the size of the needles. But most of all the texture is made by the way the yarn is knitted.

Strong and flexible

Weaving and knitting make the best use of the strength and flexibility of threads.

Whichever way you pull interlaced material it is strong, yet it stays flexible and easy to use.

Today there are many ways to interlace threads. Some are shown on this page. Try them out – you only need simple materials.

Kenyan women making baskets from hemp

Weft – the
cross strips

Basket weaving uses
long strips of bamboo.
It is easy to see how
the weft is interlaced
through the warp

Warp – the
upright strips

Weaving

Weaving uses *two* types of yarn or
other fibre – called the warp and
the weft. These are laid next to each
other, usually in parallel lines, with
warp and weft being *interlaced* to
hold them together.

Weaving was originally done by
hand on larger versions of the loom
shown below. Today weaving is
mainly done by machine.

A hand
loom

In weaving the warp is first
strung on the frame, or loom.
The weft is threaded through
the warp using a shuttle

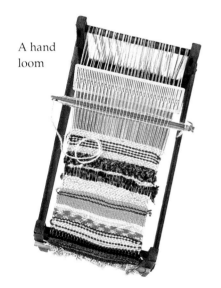

The frame that lifts
chosen pieces of yarn
is called a heddle.

The shuttle is
pushed through
after the heddle
is raised

Knots  and nets

Wherever you find a thread you are almost sure to find a knot. A knot is a way of fastening a thread to other things or to other threads. Knots make threads hold fast and they stop the ends of a thread from fraying. Knots can be used to make nets and even carpets.

Knots that hold fast
Most people find it very difficult to tie string round a parcel so that it is tight. Usually they have to get a friend to hold the first part of the knot while they make the second tie.

Surgeons have the same problem when they are stitching up skin after an operation. They have learned a trick of tying that you can try too. When you make the first part of the tie just make an extra twist. Then the knot won't slip undone while you are finishing off the tie.

How carpets take the wear
Carpets have to stand up to an enormous amount of rough treatment. First, all our weight squashes the carpet against the floor. Then, as we lift our feet, our shoes scrape the threads.

Look at a carpet in close-up and you will find it has many threads standing upright. This is called the **pile**. The threads have to be very close together so they will not flatten when walked on.

Each thread has to be knotted to a backing cloth to stop it being pulled loose by scraping feet.

Pile

Knots in backing

Fishing nets

Millions of nets are used around the world for fishing. If the net has small spaces between the threads it is called a fine **mesh**.

A fine mesh can be used to catch small fish in a pond. People who fish for a living use a coarse mesh. The net will then allow young fish to swim free, even when there are masses of nets about, as in this picture from Africa.

The net

Can you make a net?

A net looks easy to make doesn't it. But can you make a piece of fishing net like this one using some stout string? You need to practise tying the knot as shown here. It's quite easy.

How to make a knot in a net

Strong paper

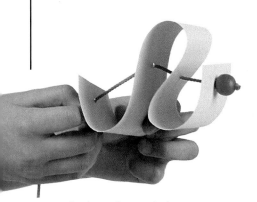

A piece of paper being pulled into a series of tight curves to make it strong

(*For more ideas on making paper strong see* Science in our World series, 'Shapes and structures')

Paper can be made very strong. The Japanese art of origami, or paper folding, uses the stiffness of paper to make beautiful models. The art of papier mache uses a combination of paper and glue to make a rock-hard modelling material.

Folding gives strength
The greetings card has a simple fold. We use it to stand the card upright when a single sheet would fall over.

The pleated or concertina folded paper is made of much thinner (tissue) paper but it will still stand up unaided. Corrugated paper uses the same idea – it is often used to protect fragile foods such as biscuits.

A box is another shape that is strong even though it is just made of folded cardboard.

Inflatable ball

The materials needed to make a papier mache bowl

Strips of coloured paper

Paste

Papier mache

This means *paper pulp* and it is made by pasting layers of paper on top of each other. Papier mache helps us see how fibres can be very strong when combined with glue.

These papier mache boxes come from Thailand. They were made by pasting lots of strips of paper over the end of a rod of wood. When the glue had dried the papier mache was taken off the wood and the rough end trimmed. Then it was painted in traditional colours and patterns. Later a lid was made for each box using the same method.

You can make your own papier mache things by using strips of coloured paper and wallpaper paste. This picture shows a bowl being made. The former for the bowl is an inflatable ball. When the bowl has dried the ball is deflated and removed. Then the top edge is trimmed.

Small Thai boxes made from papier mache. One of them has been moulded into the shape of a tortoise

The bowl after the ball has been deflated and the top edge trimmed. The inside can now be painted

(*For more ideas on papier mache see* Science in our World, 'Don't throw it away')

What wool can do

Wool has more uses than any other fibre. It is easy to obtain and poor countries can get wool as easily as rich ones.

On this page you will find some of the many things wool can do. Some may surprise you. Many properties you can check out easily for yourself. Perhaps you can even think of other things wool can do.

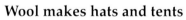

Wool makes tennis balls
Wool is strong and springy even when it has been made into felt. It makes the ideal covering for a tennis ball.

Wool makes hats and tents
Press wet wool together very hard and the scales on the fibres lock together. Now you have an almost waterproof material that is called felt. This is the stuff many types of hats are made from.

Wool felt has even been used as a housing material for some nomadic tribes in China; the felt is stretched over poles to make a warm, nearly waterproof tent.

Wool can make you itch
Wool fibres have minute scales on them arranged like the tiles on a roof. Even though the scales are very tiny they can scratch and irritate sensitive skin.

Wool makes you feel comfortable
Natural wool can take up more moisture than any other fibre. If you are hot, wool will absorb perspiration and stop you feeling wet and sweaty. Then it will slowly loose the moisture to the air.

This felted hat
is called a stetson

This shepherd from the Himalayan mountains uses wool for nearly all of his clothing.

He uses an extra blanket to keep him warm during the cold winter nights and dry when it rains.

Himalayan people do not clean the natural oil from the wool because it helps waterproof their clothing

Wool keeps you warm

Wool fibres are curly and springy and do not lie close together even after spinning. This leaves lots of room to trap air. Air trapped between fibres gives wool its insulating properties, and great warmth for little weight.

This felted hat is called a fez

Wool makes good gloves – even when wet

When wool gets wet it swells up and traps air and water, allowing the whole glove to warm up – even when they are wringing wet.

This is one reason many fishermen wear wool gloves when out at sea.

Keeping dry

A drop of water held by surface tension on a leaf

There are many ways to keep dry while on the move. Umbrellas are common, so are raincoats and parkers or anoraks. All of them are made from fabric because the fibres do not easily get wet – unless they are rubbed.

How to keep dry inside and out
Fibres are good at keeping water at bay. But people working hard in the rain can still get wet. This is because hard work causes us to sweat and give off water vapour.

The best waterproof materials have holes that are too small to let water in but big enough to let water vapour out.

Cloth pool
Most dry cloths will stop water getting through. If you take a dry dish cloth and hold it flat out beneath a tap, the water will run off the surface.

But what happens when you put a small drop of washing up liquid – it is designed to destroy **surface tension** – on another dry cloth and then try the water test again?

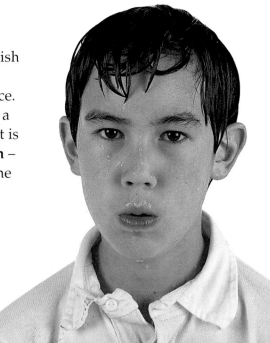

The umbrella trick

Your umbrella is made of woven fabric just like any other material and so it has gaps between the fibres. In the case of an umbrella the threads are fine and so the gaps are small. And although air and light can get through small gaps, water cannot. Watch the drops of water form on the outside of an umbrella as it rains and you will see the water stays on the surface as big blobs due to surface tension. Smooth materials are especially good at keeping out the water.

Fibres under fire

Fire happens when there is a source of heat, some air and some materials that will catch fire.

Materials are made of many sorts of fibres: some will catch fire easily. They are called **combustible** materials. Other materials are not easily combustible. Here are some reasons why.

Naturally fireproof

Animal hair is made of the same material as your finger nails. It will not burn but will simply smoulder.

By contrast, plant fibre is like wood. It will burn readily. For this reason animal hair fibres like wool are safer than plant fibres like cotton.

Astrotailoring

Astronauts have special airtight suits that are also fireproof.

The material used to fireproof a spacesuit is made from layers of closely woven glass fibres. Glass will not catch fire at all and glass fibre is extremely strong.

This is glass fibre. The direct heat from a blow torch does not make it catch fire. Instead the glass gets red hot. Because of its fire-resistance, glass fibre blankets are used to stop small kitchen fires. The blanket is thrown over the fire to stop air feeding the flames

Untreated home furnishings can catch fire easily. This picture shows a room just a couple of minutes after a smouldering cigarette caught the settee cloth on fire

Find safe fibres

It is very important to have safe fibres in the home. The fire-safe materials will usually have a label giving you this information

Look around your home for fire-safe materials. Look especially on your nightclothes, at the curtains and on the sitting room furniture. Ask a grown-up to help you search for the labels.

Weave for fire-proofing

The way that materials are made affects their resistance to fire. An open weave allows air to get to all the fibres. Closely woven materials allow less air to get at the material and they resist fire better.

Fire fighter's normal tunics are made of wool because wool is a difficult fibre to burn. The surface fibres smoulder and leave a heavy ash that protects the rest of the wool from burning.

Coatings that stop fire

All materials can be treated with special chemicals to make them safer. Fire-check chemicals are made of substances that will not catch fire. These chemicals are used to coat the surfaces of many fabrics used in the home. This reduces the chances of accidental fires.

This fireman's protective suit is made of fabrics that have been coated in special rubbers which resist heat and fire and make it waterproof and smoke-proof.

It is a good example of how it is often best to use a combination of materials to solve a problem

Dyes and colour

Colour and pattern are very important in our lives. We choose our clothes for their colours and patterns as well as their shape and size. Most fibres are naturally very dull, so to brighten them up we use many thousands of coloured substances.

A Buddhist monk in Thailand wearing a saffron-coloured robe

A natural dye can be made from squashing fruits such as the raspberries shown here

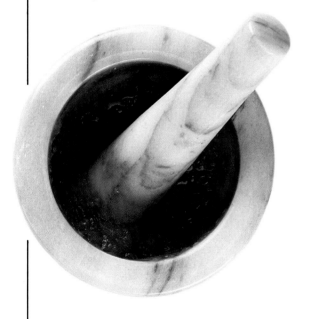

Natural colours

If you squeeze the stem of some garden plants they leave a stain on your fingers. But the stain, or **dye**, is not always the green colour you might expect. The stain from tomato plants, for example, is yellow.

The oldest types of dyes come from the twigs, leaves, roots, berries and flowers of plants. Saffron, for example, is a yellow-orange dye that is made from the central parts of a crocus.

A few dyes come from animals. Cochineal is a red dye that comes from small Mexican insects.

Dyed skeins hung
up to dry in Morocco

Dipping dyes

Fibres are usually dyed after they have been spun into yarn. The skeins are then dipped into vats of hot dye, and then hung up to dry. In some countries the dyeing is done in the street, making a very colourful scene. Most modern cloth dyeing has to be done in a factory because man-made materials need to be dyed at very high temperatures.

Man-made colours

It is very difficult to make good dyes from plants. Today nearly all dyes are made artificially, many of them from oil.

Making a dye in a chemical factory makes sure that the same colour can be made time and time again. Artificial, or synthetic, dyes are also valuable because they rarely fade.

Uniform but different

Dyes can be used to give striking colours that can be used to make people easier to see.

Dyes can also be used to camouflage people who wish to stay hidden. The patterns of green and brown dyes used on a soldier's battle dress make the soldier much more difficult to spot when fighting in leafy countryside.

Uniforms and flags are often designed to be readily seen.

Colours and patterns

A piece of a jumper that uses several different kinds of stitch and coloured yarns to create patterns and textures

There are some wonderful patterns in nature. The blotchy pattern of a giraffe is used for camouflage. The striped yellow and black pattern of a wasp is used as a warning. People have copied natural patterns in their clothes, but they've invented some totally new ones too.

Printing
The easiest way to get a coloured pattern on a cloth is to print it in a printing press. The cloth first goes through a printing press where a colour is stamped on to it from a roller. Then it moves on to more rollers each with a different colour until the pattern is complete.

Printing can produce any pattern you want. It can make both delicate patterns and some very bold and striking ones.

Knitted patterns
Many strands of yarn can be used in very complicated patterns such as the one shown here. The pattern depends on knitting loops so that each coloured yarn shows on the surface only when needed; otherwise the yarns loop unseen across the back of the knitting.

HASIRA ZA MKIZI TIJARA YA MVUVI

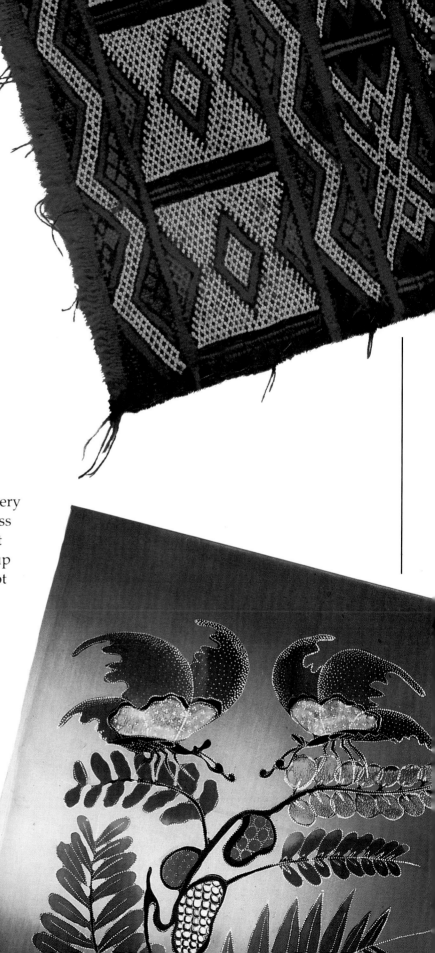

Weaving

Pattern is added to a weave by changing the coloured yarns as they are push through the warp by the shuttle (see page 26).

More pattern can be created by threading the weft through different numbers of warp threads. You may spot how that is done in this picture.

Batik

Dyes can be used to make very striking effects. In the process called Batik, the cloth is first painted with wax to cover up the areas of cloth that are not to be dyed. When the cloth is placed in the dye bath the waxed areas remain uncoloured. Then the cloth is boiled to melt away the wax.

Batiks have many colours and each colour needs the same wax treatment. It takes a long time to make a batik, but the result is very striking.

Tie dying

Creating pattern with dye depends on getting some parts of the cloth to take the dye while others remain untouched. Several ways of doing this have been shown on the previous page. However, it is easy to experiment with making patterns and, at the same time, to investigate how cloth takes up dye.

Tie dying is a traditional technique of adding colour and pattern to a cloth using the simplest of materials.

Dyes add colour wherever they are absorbed by the cloth

Dipping the knotted cloth in dye

Tying a tight knot using string

Tie dyeing

Sometimes it is nice to be surprised by the dye pattern. In tie dying you never really know what effect you are going to get.

The first step in tie dyeing is to tie knots in the cloth. The dye cannot get into the knot properly. When the cloth is taken from the dye bath and the knots undone, all kinds of interesting patterns are found. See if you can experiment to get the patterns you want.

Tying a loose knot in the cloth

The tie-dyed cloth after it has been hung out to dry

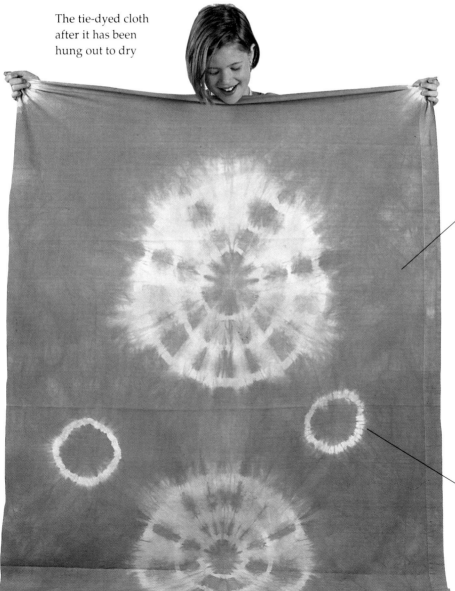

How the dye seeps into the loose knot

The dye is kept cleanly away using tight string binding

43

Clothes for all seasons

The world is full of clothes. Most of them are mass produced and look the same. But in the past people made clothes for themselves.

Traditional dress is very beautiful and it is also practical. People did not make clothes for show, they made them to match the weather conditions.

Here we show you some traditional clothes and tell you the weather they were made for. For contrast we also show you some of the newest types of dress – also geared to the weather.

Staying warm
Some parts of the world are very cold and the people that live in these areas have learned to cope by wearing animal furs or by wrapping up in thick woollen clothes.

This lady is from Mongolia in Asia, a country that has very cold winters.

Keeping cool
Cotton clothes are the choice of this person from India. In her country the weather is hot all year round and the main problem is keeping cool. Light cotton can also be dyed into colourful patterns.

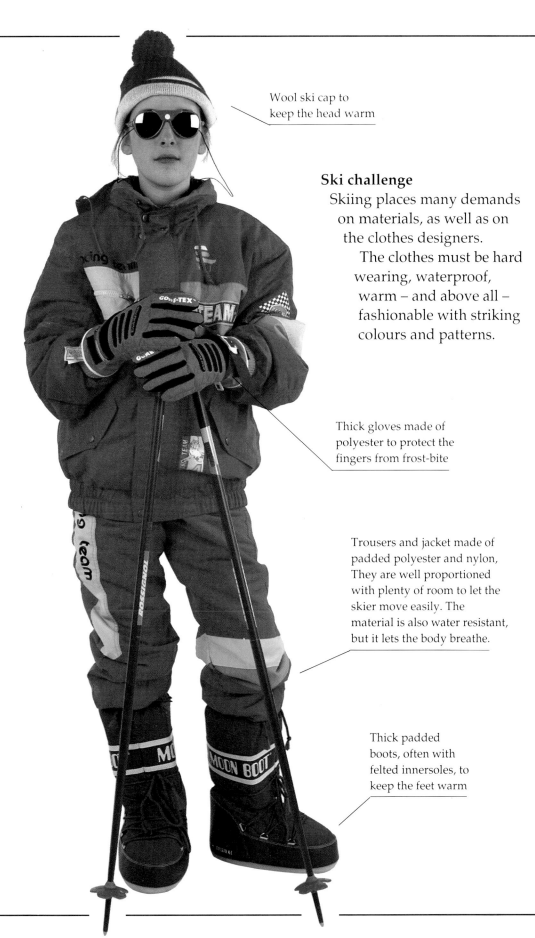

Wool ski cap to
keep the head warm

Ski challenge
Skiing places many demands
on materials, as well as on
the clothes designers.
    The clothes must be hard
wearing, waterproof,
warm – and above all –
fashionable with striking
colours and patterns.

Thick gloves made of
polyester to protect the
fingers from frost-bite

Trousers and jacket made of
padded polyester and nylon,
They are well proportioned
with plenty of room to let the
skier move easily. The
material is also water resistant,
but it lets the body breathe.

Thick padded
boots, often with
felted innersoles, to
keep the feet warm

New words

camouflage
a pattern of colours designed to blend in with the surroundings

carding
the process which gets the natural fibres pulled out into line, removes the seeds and other small pieces of unwanted material

cells
our bodies are made of millions of small building blocks called cells. Each cell has a special job. In places where hair grows, cells are made and then organised into long rods (hair) which are gradually pushed out of the skin.

cocoon
a silky envelope which protects the silkworm as it changes from a caterpillar to a moth. The silkworm gradually wraps itself in silk by pushing out a long continuous thread from a special place on its body

combustible
a material that can burn is said to be combustible. Three conditions are needed for combustion: the material, a source of heating such as a match, and a supply of air

dye
a staining or colouring chemical. Natural dyes have been used for thousands of years, but it is difficult to get a complete range of colours. Artificial, or synthetic, dyes are often made from oil

fabric
a cloth made from fibres by knitting, weaving, felting and a variety of other processes

felting
a special process of matting wool, cotton and other materials so they make a dense waterproof material. Felting is done using both heat and pressure

fibre
a natural or synthetic strand, or filament, of material that may be spun into a thread. There are many fibres that are used in fabrics, from the thin strands of glass that make fibre-glass to the delicate fibres off sheep and goats that make wool

fleece
the coat of wool that covers a sheep or goat. The wool is not naturally straight, but has a natural crinkly shape which stands up even after it has become wet. A fleece is also covered with natural oils to help keep the hairs waterproof

fur
the coat of fine hairs that cover many animals such as cats and dogs. Fur has the same purpose as the fleece of a sheep; it helps to keep the animal warm and dry

mesh
the name given to the size of holes left when a net is made. The size of the mesh is very important in fishing nets, for example, because a big or coarse mesh allows small fish to escape and continue to grow

pile
the yarns of a fabric that stand up from the surface of the fabric. Velvet and carpets have a pile. In the case of carpets the pile is made by looping many yarns through a backing sheet

polyester
a range of synthetic fibres made originally from oil. Polyester fibres are very springy, so they will always try to spring back to their original straight shape. This is what makes polyesters resist creasing

pores
the surface of the skin has many tiny holes in it. These holes are called pores. Some pores allow fluids, such as sweat, to flow out, others – follicles – provide openings for growing hair

skein
a length of yarn that has been wound into a long coil. Skeins are useful ways of storing yarns. Knitting wool is often sold in skeins

spinning
the process of twisting fibres of wool, cotton, hemp and other short fibres together so that they give a long thread or yarn which can then be used to make fabrics. Long fibres such as silk are not spun, but simply wound together to give threads

surface tension
a special property of liquids which makes the surface of a liquid look and behave as though it had an invisible skin over the surface

tease
the process of gently pulling at a matted collection of fibres so they become loosened and then can be separated. Teasing is an essential first step in spinning

textile
the general name for any kind of fabric or cloth, but especially when it has been woven

woven (to weave)
the interlacing of threads or yarn to form an interlaced pattern that will not fall apart. This process is still done by hand in many countries, but it can also be done very swiftly by machine. A weaving frame was one of the first machines that started the industrial revolution over two hundred years ago

yarn
a continuous twisted strand of fibres produced by a process such as spinning

Index